I0797677

CORD SWELL

CORD SWELL

Poems

brittny ray crowell

W. W. NORTON & COMPANY
Independent Publishers Since 1923

Printed in the United States of America
First Edition

For information about permission to reproduce selections from this book, write to Permissions, W. W. Norton & Company, Inc., 500 Fifth Avenue, New York, NY 10110

For information about special discounts for bulk purchases, please contact W. W. Norton Special Sales at specialsales@wwnorton.com or 800-233-4830

Manufacturing by Lakeside Book Company
Book design by Chris Welch
Production manager: Louise Mattarelliano

ISBN 978-1-324-11115-3

W. W. Norton & Company, Inc., 500 Fifth Avenue, New York, NY 10110
www.wwnorton.com

W. W. Norton & Company Ltd., 15 Carlisle Street, London W1D 3BS

$PrintCode

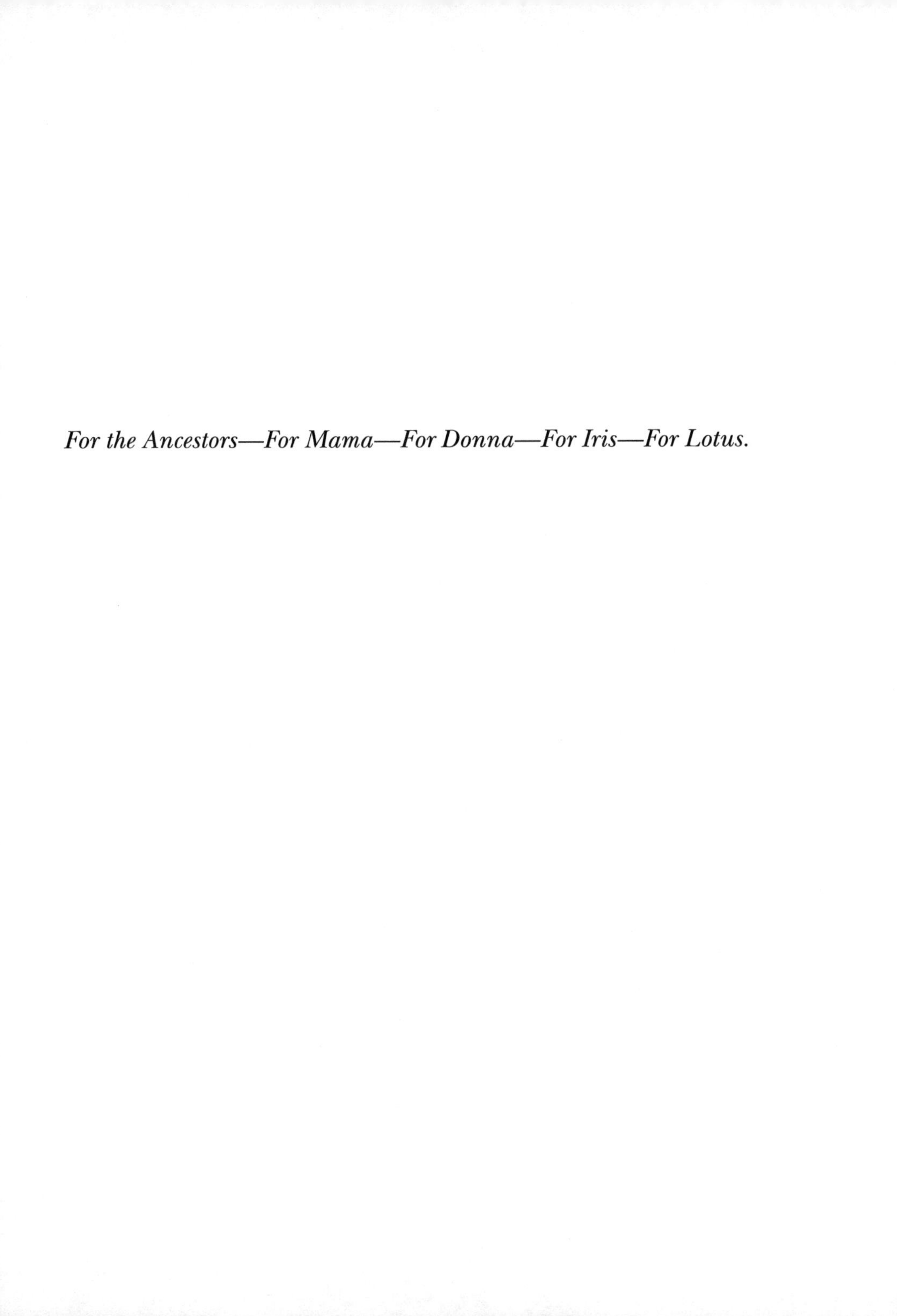

For the Ancestors—For Mama—For Donna—For Iris—For Lotus.

CONTENTS

III.

IV.

CORD SWELL

I'M NOT HERE TO TALK ABOUT THE RATS OR ROACHES

only that we were not a nasty people
but this is what we could afford:

a little place in the shade. a little roof over our heads to pray
and give thanks the water didn't seep into our beds or kitchens
when it rained   that the creek didn't rise to crown
our sleeping skulls   good lord

that we didn't serve a god who pursed his lips at mercy
but who give us this day to study something silent in a cul de sac of pine
that he give us the joy to feel nestled as a jaybird bathing in somebody's palm

i can do all things by persimmon   by the gold glint
of fireflies shining off gilded teeth   by the brown
ashy limbs of cousins packed in a ford f-150

i can do all things by Puddin
Butcherknife   &   Poochie
by the blood of Jesus   &   the Bud Ice in the cooler

i can do all things by our mothers who knew
how to patchwork a pallet for us to rest
our heads just high enough from up off the ground
who worked this stingy crumb of good earth
into cabbage & tomatoes wide as a baby's brow

but where are all those names
sweet as the caramel & red velvet of yesteryear?

where did they go   the JohnnieMaes
the Dorothys   the Gracies?

I.

they shall
be walk, and not

he Omnipotent power of God

faint.

Gal. 5: 22 - But the fruit
love, joy, peace, lo
ness, goodness, fa
temperance: agai
no law.

Isa

The unmerited favor of God or
the underserved favor of God is
describing grace.

Eclipse

i’m gonna collect every word

you ever spoke   & put them in a box

somewhere   then one day let them fly

like a chorus of moths landing on brown

tree branches

Interview with an Ancestor I

Are you alone?
i was reared in a Christian home with a godly mother
and grandparents who gave me Christian guidance

i truly believed that God died for my sins—i never doubted this
i always believed that God, through his mercy, would forgive me

Do you miss me?
we may know God, but what i'm here to talk about is suffering

i sift for stars through the crown shyness of trees
baiting my line, fishing for a crescent moon

What motivates you more, fear or love?
i've shed something into each of you
a beautiful unspooling

when i went under
i could see an intricate beauty

Do you sleep? And if so, do you dream?
the worst development is that i can no longer keep things from you

Choose one: night or day?
to love the Lord with all my heart, strength, mind and soul
and my fellow man as myself—this fulfilled the void i lacked in my life

nevertheless, there was still something missing—a certain yearning
i couldn't grasp or comprehend

Nurse's Log

i will be here one hour and thirty mins

my bottom is breaking down
she is sore from all that turning   my skin is bones

my open mouth

and I gave her shallow cup of juice.

i will not let death take me
sleeping   i watch

memory flutter like a swarm
of monarchs   a flicker
of fireflies forming the almond
of my mother's eye again
    a cornflower for an iris
    an exit i can run through

she nurses me with medicine, oatmeal, and prayer
whispers in the quiet room of herself

god
if this don't work   take her

save the soul tethered
to a body ruined

send her dervishing back to light

Down 59

speak *home*, and watch memory surface in the air
like a hologram. watch ground
flatten to make room for sky. watch sound
simmer to syrup as one man begs in the ear
of another man's wife. pause until you hear
a sluice of ice inside a can tilted down
like an hourglass for your aunt that craves the burn of cold. now drown
the familiar. hold it below like a fish too small to keep. prepare

for the flood that washes you back onto your mother's doorstep
before the tide comes and claims you as its own
speak *home*, and watch memory splinter into clover
watch as your hands spin shadows into silk webs
translucent and thin
but broad enough to cross over

The Ladder Is Always There

remember the Christmas your mother climbed
the dusty orchard of the attic searching

for ornaments   her soft feet stepping
like each rung wouldn't betray

her   like each one was a bone
in a column of the back of someone who loved her

only it wasn't the ladder but the ceiling
that broke her   imagine your mother falling

through sheetrock while you are sleeping
(what is the sound of someone landing

while you dream ?)   with only a basket to break
her fall   how she had to crawl across the ugly

avocado green garage into the house to call
for help   how she never woke

you from her bed
to save you from the memory

ribs, meat

Blood Petition: A Prayer of Reckoning

the house quaked by the gods
lacks no form of disaster
creeping after all the clan

—*Antigone*

Dear Blood,

the answers filled like pails when the gods rained fire towards our home. this fight was unfair—unevenly yoked—all we had were our hands and our tongues twisted towards song to save us against their wrath. what's left relies on your discretion. please choose.

would you rather:

- ❏ the chaos come on sunday, so close to christmas you can hardly tell the colored lights from the flames. the sky turns red with cherry embers. so silent is the night that the baby sleeps, swaddled in darkness, resting against rising screams.

- ❏ a plague of spirits on your houses. a sea of fists stoning the walls you built.

- ❏ your gardens shot with salt. nothing here will ever grow. there is too much dying to weed. the soil sours over the remnants of the seeds you planted, and the children are hungry, so very hungry, with no turnips to pull, no weeping breasts to root their mouths against.

- ❏ the walls of the altars grow silent. *the rituals fail to take.* there is no space for new names, though we crowd them.

- ❏ and we are lonely.

your prompt reply is requested. everything relies on your discretion.

kindly,
we, the living

Answer: All of the above. The answers overlap. One hurt bleeds into the next. You fail. There is no consolation. There will be no retakes. You lose.

Mama Voice

you see, we all start out as haints. wispy

shadowy vapory things—that part comes first.

when you think of them there, you have to think of yourself there, too

no matter that you're above and they're below.

it's the same, like an hourglass. you're

trickling down and they're receiving.

it's all divisible, like silt from bone—

bone becomes weakened, weathered, eaten

down like a stick of chalk until it's carried off into clouds,

coats your hands like a soft, silky thing you can't pick up

it transfers off to all the things you touch, those you pine

for and those you loathe

you have to believe that it's happening to you here

even now, in this very place you call home

Fasss

for Mama belly pooched like a teacake
seventeen years old thrust
towards the congregation framed
by stained glass deacon eyes
that nicked at her legs fix
on her lips as she says *i'm sorry*

months pass
the young absent father
mumbles *sorry my mama*
says i have to go to school
he tucks the baby's picture in his wallet
grins *but she look just like me*

*

for all the times i was out
"hunching" never in your house
—only once all the times my body
shamed me for the friction of boys
that felt so good over clothes

*

to you mannish heifa
heathened hoes that grew
too good too soon faster
than your girlhood
all pig-tailed and big-hipped
swollen-breasted and wide-behinded

to Big Mama beneath gray eyes
already too old from gestating
the vision of your rape
the baby's name a breadcrumb
begging towards truth   a name
a good family swore you wouldn't
tell against   a man called
by god the best
of us—our kind   your cousin.

to little ones laid to sleep
on dark backroom beds
at family functions
every touch you
won't remember

to little boys   grown woman
on your baby bird lips
congratulation slaps
on your bony boy back
from men who call you lucky

to mothers wishing to peel
the rind of men from their breasts
praying their babies ugly/stunted
pleading a spell of safety
from lurking gazes   praying
for a god that sees the future
this time   and finally answers

II.

Red Bird

Interview with an Ancestor II

Where's your soul?
live from the eigengrau

How do you show me you love me?
and can't annn one of you niggas whoop me

If you could do anything differently, what would it be?
i have not reached perfection—but i am striving towards that goal

What's it like to die?
a grease   a salve

Do you sleep? And if so, do you dream?
nevertheless, there was still something missing—a certain yearning
or something i couldn't grasp or comprehend

What was your first memory?
i kind of clung to him and told him i'd been trapped in an elevator
once before

Do you miss being here?
the dead men under the live oak playing pitty pat and dominoes

What are the contents of your dreams?
you may find me in a palace with a wraparound porch
solid sapphire card tables built right into the floor

every plant and flower has a name
after those who love us and who we show love through care

we place them in a stream of sunlight when the sky is clear
and under the water the roof catches when it rains

Things You Put in a Crown Royal Bag While Playing Dominoes

six is the spinner
the summer your auntie is given a pistol
swaddled in purple flannel
by her brother   your play uncle
out on the porch

he holds a row of white slabs in both hands
like harmonicas   studies them like damage
after a storm

niggas love to play crazy   you show him
crazy when you light his black
ass up like a christmas tree

he throws the bones down on the table
with a thunder that makes your eyes flinch

three-eyed ella   she does what i tella
tin top   roof don't leak

To the Tune of What's a Telephone Bill by Bootsy Collins (Pt. I)

i saw you standing by the punchbowl at the party all quiet like. you didn't have enough ass to make a po man a sandwich but i saw you dancing your black velvet glo against the red light and said that'll do for tonight

Side A

01. every woman i wanted	1:26
02. was like new money burning	1:46
03. a hole in my pocket	1:54
04. i couldn't wait	2:17
05. to get a hold of you	0:42
06. just to turn around	0:47
07. and give you away	1:09

To the Tune Of What's a Telephone Bill by Bootsy Collins (Pt. II)

a body is just a sleight of hand. that's what my eyes told you while you watched me dance. there's only so much magic a man can have before he breaks. a body is just a sleight of hand

Side B

01. i needed a softness	0:23
02. to be bruised	0:34
03. by the underside of tongue	0:42
04. here i am baby	0:47
05. standing at the corner of wait-	1:00
06. lessness/sans	1:30
07. fear	0:34
08. *you inspire me (to poetry)*	0:20
09. *let me breathe*	3:05
10. all my ache	0:34
11. back into your ear	4:09

To the Tune of Give Me Your Love (Love Song) by Curtis Mayfield

he liked his women black with hair shorter than a click on a 45, women he felt he could beat so he could love on them later while listening to music, the crooning grooving into his strokes, curving like hooks as their legs held him like a necklace clasp at the scoop of his back

Side A

01. eye contact (is)	1:28
02. another way to obey	1:32
03. another way to make a body	1:34
04. stay and play dead	1:36
05. look me in my eyes	1:50
06. when I'm loving you	1:58
07. don't you run from it	1:28

Side B

01. when I'm loving you (extended version)	1:32
02. girl don't turn away	1:34

03. bitch don't you know 1:36

04. i could break you 1:28

To the Tune of Why Have I Lost You by Cameo

I.

i had plenty of time to breathe
against the powder settling in your twilight

scent and didn't   baby   i'm trying
to save you from the memory

II.

it must of gut you like a cool fish   baby
it must of spit in your snuff juice

colored eyes to see   to come claim me
from up under another

woman   i won't act like i didn't know
how far i was from home
and where running away was to   baby

III.

look   baby   i'm trying
to spread my face across your chest

to worry the holes beneath your collarbones
to study a while   a maple buckeye

of nipple   like a sundial   don't you

treat me   like no dead dog loose
and hit in the road

IV.

the same face you made when you cried
is the same face you made when we fucked

only now i see the difference
your moaning mouth from your mourn

each one forms a different hole

V.

loving you was like a small thing mouthing
a sweet crumb   bigger than a belly could hold

Victuals

i love you like sugar water
like the syrup in my milk or the sandwich
you made with one slice of bread

folded over in my hand   the sticky amber
peeking out like a horizon   i love you
like sardines smothered in oil and funk

in the can   how they nestled together
so tightly   remember the surprise of finding
one tucked up under another

how our hunger left us wading
through an emulsion of hot sauce and bones
i love your hands patting a pulp of water

and cornmeal like a snowball
how you sacrificed your skin
to grease to get the golden crisp

on the outside just right
i love your fingers stripping membrane
from shit   the wash and repeat of it

for me to taste only a sliver
of chittlin   your fork floating
towards my opened mouth   your hand

held under my chin like a basin
some things you can only trust
from the palms of those who love you

those who would forage the forest's edge
or some small patch by the road
for dandelion   poke sallet   anything God

made most folk had overlooked
but we remembered could kill
hongry if handled with care   i love you

because you first loved me like pickled eggs
and penny candy   like pot likker on a baby's breath

i love you to the point of sopping
i forget feeling full

Scar Elegy

they sealed your wound with butterfly closures
a kaleidoscope flew up your face for weeks

the wings were supposed to hold you
as you healed   better than needle
and thread that couldn't suture you

smooth but the wings still left a long shallow
groove that never filled

*

now that the earth is over you   (a safety)
i take the long way home across your face
map the architecture of your blood
and pray against dying early

by the hands of a man who makes a craft of loving
women like dogs   a man who tames
with heavy petting and violence
who mistakes sweetness for something soft to carve

"Your Navel Cord's Well"
—D.L.M. (1960–2019)

in my quiet time
i whisper you to emerge.

i bagged your pillows in plastic
tried to trap your venom
like wasps in clear jars

studied how to cultivate
your scent:

something like the musk of menthols
mixed with syrup or sugar water—

but who can tell now?

you left me
no potions to do this.

*

i've never summoned anything
from the soil like rain

if only i could loosen a tomb

from red clay like milk teeth
from soft pink jaw

i am not a god
that questions
who she made to destroy
who am i
to meddle the earth?

*

today is another distance—
your voice plaits
through my core

your ash settles in some vessel
on a dusty shelf

this hurt is a bulge—

my belly bursts a bull's eye
open from sealed husk again

*

if there's any such thing
as paradise   some aftervoid
better than the warmth
of your neck, the sun swept
slab of your porch,

with you there, *the map*
of your palm waving—
how close am i
to that context of space?

where am i now with this mouth
—an infant
red bird wailing

whose song is this
with your ear turned
from my tongue

and where does its echo
call home?

you're too heavy for cocoons
no hull to hold you

Origin Tongues

1 your tongue was my tongue
stacking towers
over Babel
probing the city of god

2 *they* troubled the mortar between *us*

3 we carved our names
into sky

4 your name fell from my mouth
and scattered

5 all the ways i used to worship
you

6 we have no words for now

III.

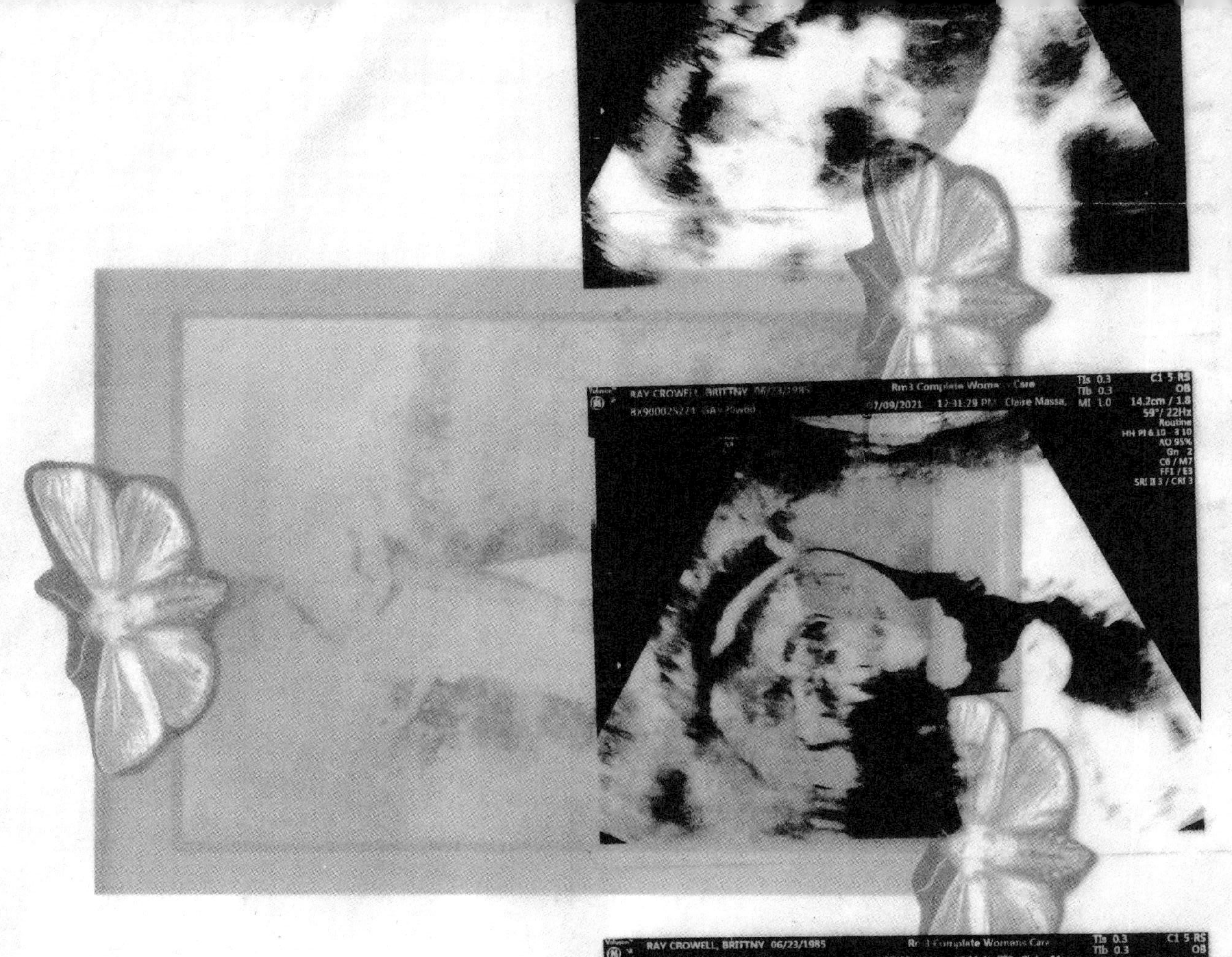
RAY CROWELL, BRITTNY 06/23/1985
Complete Womens Care
07/09/2021 12:31:29 PM Claire Massa,
TIs 0.3
TIb 0.3
MI 1.0
C1 5 RS
OB
14.2cm / 1.8
59°/ 22Hz
Routine
AO 95%
Gn 2
C6 / M7
FF1 / E3
SRI II 3 / CRI 3
RAY CROWELL, BRITTNY 06/23/1985
Complete Womens Care
8X900025274 GA=20w6d
Claire Massa,
TIs 0.3
TIb 0.3
MI 1.0
C1 5 RS
OB
14.2cm / 1.1
59°/ 22Hz
Routine
AO 95%
Gn 3
C6 / M7
FF1 / E3

Interview with an Ancestor III

How do you show me you love me?
i can think of many failures
one of which is that i can't make gravy

When were you born?
night is where we let others find us finding ourselves

how many things have i seen that i did not see
impressed with my own magic?

Do you hurt?
your mouth clamps over my breast like a tiny oyster
your sister's tooth, purged just last week, rests on the corner of my night-
stand   she doesn't think of any fairies for once   so it sits there in its
buttery eggshell
a speck of rot had been forming and i wonder over all the small worries
what moment of indulgence i allowed that led to this decay

Where is your soul?
honeysuckle   chunking chinaberries   dead frogs   coal oil   catching wasps in
jars of coal oil   pulling the heads off grasshoppers   snakes warning   birds
chirping   letting you know when snakes are near   burning up the grass   Big
Mama hollering   making sure it didn't go into the white folks' yard

Jesus and dairy queen   and pleasant grove   Big Mama's stockings knotted
at the knee   and her housecoats   and ajax   and tom and jerry on the zenith
or the curtis mathes tv   HenryCharles and his horses   the flat land   danger
and imagination   and tape recordings of fake scenes   chittlins and shelling

peas and pecans   fighting with cousin Todd   chasing him around the house
with a butcher knife

home is a complicated place

What's it like where you are?
i confessed Jesus Christ as my savior at an early age

this lasted for years

he makes it sound like i'm begging

Do you remember touch?
i began to take on new perceptions

a benign milk-filled cyst

echoes reanimating

How can I find you when I need you the most
i cut my hair to the scalp like a swimmer
so the tension wouldn't weigh me down

shame has its own language
a noiseless uncalled for

What is your name?
i'm just not sure

i tend to wander
wanting to be
consumed and seen

If you could do anything differently, what would it be?
i hardened myself like the husk of a seed
as if what troubled me had the potential to grow
beyond me

first of our Arkansas grandmother's flesh
blood of our grandfathers

are you still here?

Husks or the Cryptic Call of Cicada (Exo)skeletons

nothing lasts that long—not the elder-
berry stain on your palm

not the taste seeping
beneath your cobblestone tongue

not even the smell of unburied hair
still greased   resting in your brush like a silk nest

and still i hold to the half life
of you   every head womb
of memory my morning warmth

maybe one day there'll be someone
bending my voice back
like the spine of a sapling

someone straining to strangle
my scent out of some garment
wringing my name like a rag

32 Teeth

monday:
picture me in the aperture
20 years not old
enough to drink what i mixed
behind the bar   20 years from my mother's breast
is a lifetime in the gaze

of a man that could be my daddy's friend
says he'll take his old fashioned
down the crease of my spine
asks how did i get my skin
to trap the light like that says it kills
him to see a pretty thing he can't break
quickly as his wife comes back from changing
the baby he tells me later should have been ours

friday:
white man in a Mister Rogers sweater
holding a camera comes early
on my shift saying he's taking pictures
for a calendar of the little
five points neighborhood would i like
to be a part of it

i bend to his direction
i ask if i could be june
my birth month he says all days any days
for a smile like mine tells me
fold your arms like this across the counter

that's it such a stunning girl
the way you wear your hair so natural
you look like you could be foxy
brown straight from the seventies, girl

i picture my shoulders smoothing the angles
of his lens   brown light bending
kaleidoscopic   picture my mother hanging me
against the wall waiting for my month to come like a horizon
i always told you you should model always
knew someone would discover you baby

two weeks: he hands me my face
in a brown envelope
two photos: one with me better than i've ever seen
before my head haloed by bar lights
and cocktail glasses, mouth like a palette of pearl
the second the same save for my breasts
bulboused   pixelated   (re)imagined

dolloped on the surface like dough left to rise
i remember the arch of my smile bending higher
when he said *oh you can do better than that for me   smile*
like you really mean it   smile
like the whole world will see it

two weeks: mama asks for the day
the calendar's coming
oh   Mama   he never came back

Notes on Your Absence

i saged the house when you left
turns out memories are immune to ash

i could ask why and other questions
like what is the sound of bruising—

your blue black face kneaded under god's
sore thumbs waiting to be made anew?

what i mean to say is that i'm sorry
Mama says she's gotta have a life too

she can't mend a man she loves from his own
silt—can't hush a small hive of noise swarming

the snow globe of your jail cell
can't release all the things you imagine

you see from being real
your mind is strong

and more brutal than the two hands
you never knew could kill

by raising a man up to light
to see through him

Place pecans in pastry shell. Cool slightly sugar

pecan halves 1 C 1 tsp. Ground Cinnamon

1½ cups light

packets, bring

Dash salt

½ to 1 tsp

Method:

Meanwhile, Combine

lemon juice, Cinnamon,

Bring to boil.

3 slightly beaten eggs

7 lbs beef back ribs

3/4 cup water

1 teaspoon vanilla

Down 7th, Over East St.

ten years felt long enough to avoid
that road, the one near the tracks paved thick
and high, a swollen keloid
two lanes of magical black isthmus
cleaving the seas of two states
tingling with a phantom
humiliation you can't soothe. guilt becomes a part of your face
you can't even fathom
how you'd look without the girth of worry bloated
under your eyelids like a fat egg sac
you've known the weight too long not to hold it
it's too late to bring it back

to pass on for another to foster as their own
when you are the body it calls home

How to Play Dead (Again)

Inspired by Jamaica Kincaid's "Girl." Dedicated to Charleston (amend as necessary)

I.

beware of "black" suffixes
restrict your syllables like haiku
name the child so they bear witness
to words planted against
them like a rancid kiss
lest your children
become the sluts or thugs
they believe we are
so bent on becoming

II.

still your violent tongues
maim your swarthy mouths
even your silence
is angry—

smile wide—prove you are not dangerous
—bring the corners of your broad mouth in tight
display a great lunette of moon-varnished teeth

make your eyes soft
and vacant though they are dark

III.

bow
your head. offer the swirling dark
serifs of your temples
the grapevines of your dark
thistled "kitchen" above
your neck—tilt
your eyes to earth
make yourself still
pretend that you are willing
discomfort is rude and dangerous
better petted than bruised—
laugh at your own expense

learn to carry your eyes
like hailstorms, your throat
a tourniquet, running the chasms
of your noxious blood backward
swallow all the words
you want to say but can't

IV.

hug no man/woman/child
you love for fear your arms
may crave embrace—pray
without getting shot

know there is no such play
as safe—make yourself small
infinitesimal, fetal as a curl
reason with your scourge—pretend
you know what it is to be lovable
bounce a ball
gospel a song

V.

make room for younger ancestors
this world is for those too old
for death's childish palette

VI.

but what if i'm too dense to bow
too stubborn to swoon?

well—if all else fails, chile
—when they come for you

set a kettle—
hear the rising fume scream

—imagine your courteous death

A Tether

my sister is shedding the virus
i imagine her from within
like a snow globe   olio of blood
and the thing that could have killed her
snowflakes sloughing sickness like skin

i think of all the men my body hosted
wonder if i'm still peeling
their touch from the inside like glue

what is the half life of bodies
tethered   how long to keep
a bird's nest left empty

imagine me grating under the grooves
of their fingers   winding
into corkscrews of ribbon
for wind to catch   for ground to settle
for grass to mend
into mingled debris
how long to purge
imprints unseen   the damage
absorbed within me

in the stained glass of my memory
i picture peach meat under dark bark exposed
my fat bottomed heart in their palms

Granny Had a Open Face Gold Front

—after Wanda Coleman

why   yo mama name you
so white   why   you so little
why   you try to dance and

ain't got enough ass
to make a po man
a sandwich   why you can't take
a damn joke   why you always reading
books and shit   why you still in school
don't you get tired   why you don't give
that man another baby
why you so selfish
      you was?   when?
well   damn   i'm sorry hell
how was i supposed to know you was pregnant then
you know
everythinghappensforareasonbaby

when you coming back to church
you know you not too good to go to hell
do yo daddy know you cuss like that
how you a school teacher
drinking and smoking blacks
you too pretty for that

when   you coming back
        home

how come you don't call
yo granny no mo

A Good Thing Found

prepare yourself
for entry

prime yourself to be stripped
like something ripe
and swaddled in soft velvet
never mind how the skin feels

peeling
the body will yield
remember you are claimed for

this plucking
open yourself
make way for whatever may bloom

you are ground
you are soil
you are earth

that makes men's hands
black from hard work
you are fostered

by roots/fortified by bone
and the filth of dying
never mind the blood
left behind
yield to me/something new

prepare yourself for planting
take what you are given and shit
for me a diamond

splinter yourself into a head
of white petals/i want to see
the flowers crowning
i want to see/your lips
splayed like an orchid's skull

give me something
to admire/give me something
i can name/after

the way/a body
splits/like the edges
of a maple leaf rotting/give me something

my love/can suture
give me some
thing i can claim

A Cleaving

today i make my tea
with the vanilla soy milk you left

it clouds the cup
like the birth of a star
embraced in porcelain
like the dissipating
breath a drop of blood
makes in clear water

when you come to me you leave
things a tapestry of stains
in the shape of recognizable things

woman who left her blood
in my bed as a goodbye
like a note in a rocking chair

take yourself with you—
leave no trails like a slug

i carry the scent of you
on my hands for days
struggle to make a fist
to pound your skeletons
to ash and powder

you are the word caught sideways
in the tender pink of my throat

a baby plunked in the neighbor's
drinking well like a coin
my breast weeping milk as i walk away

What Were You Wearing

after the survivors' exhibits of the same name

they asked me what i was wearing
a t-shirt jeans and dirty converse
a pink and gold silk sari
a hospital gown under sterile sheets
an army combat uniform and a gun
a practice football jersey tights and cleats
a velvet ivory choir robe
a neon bedazzled g string and clear heels
flannel pajamas and a satin hair bonnet
a diaper

a diaper
flannel pajamas and a satin hair bonnet
a neon bedazzled g string and clear heels
a velvet ivory choir robe
a practice football jersey tights and cleats
an army combat uniform and a gun
a hospital gown under sterile sheets
a pink and gold silk sari
a t-shirt jeans and dirty converse
they asked me what i was wearing

The Women I

when there were no
more cups
we drank from each
other's skulls
reflected on each other's
breasts like sundials
i will forever be
counseled by the
groove down your back
the place sap is
released from pine trees
to make the hollow
of your earrings glow

do you remember
when we swung on
the front porch and
i asked
"what would a flower
give another flower"
and you said
"a bee"

if i had been an orchid
i would have covered
your bath with
lavender ears
like van gogh

Let Me Tell You All the Things My Broken Body's Been

a tomb
a bomb
a bloom in a vestibule for violence

once i dreamed a body pristine
a cistern full of holy water
a road where a young girl
wanders unnoticed
forgets she's been
so far without fear

i never asked to be clover
tender hearted   hunted and plucked
let me be sprawling like the kudzu
for once   let me smother
what would take me over

lord prepare me
to be a sanctuary
a succor for love

The Women II

oh how we laughed
to find our plums
filled with fruit flies
our sun full of black girls
with limbs
like king snakes

oh your eyes that
lynched the light
like murderers

i wear your hands
as the clasp of my favorite
necklace the one that
drapes long with eggshell
orbs spit straight from
your full mouth

IV.

Interview with an Ancestor IV

Do you ever close your eyes and pretend it's 1985? 1996? We were wrong about time all along, weren't we? How long will you keep this to yourself?

because you said poke sallet. because the creek and elm. because the Fish Man with the light green hazel eyes. because the house in Macedonia with JuJu and the Brileys to the right and Ms. Toot and Scootie to the left. because your auntie and my auntie played cards friday nights through the fog of seneca menthol lights. because together is a mighty long time after all. because absence from the body, baby, is not without a home. the light is on. the light is on.

Who named you? Would you rename yourself if you could? Have you?

honeysuckle
coal oil

dead frogs
bird song

chinaberry
flat land

benediction
pecan

danger
imagination

windmill cookies
and a wedge of hoop cheese

After all this time, how do I know it's you?
keep on living

what one child won't remember
the other one will in fragments

i don't believe in second chances
i believe in the process of unfurling

my illness is that i try to imagine something beautiful
about everyone who did me wrong

the answer to prayer is to send your ache flying
the sky buoyancy of bird bones

the one who sent me used to sit lotus position
on the counter picking her chin for silk stems

this is an exercise in holding
breath   of knowing what to save and what to release

you say you want more of this life
when you've barely had it on your tongue

i taught you everything you know
but none of what i've left behind

watch and keep on living

I Dreamed My Name in Your Mouth with Pink Flowers

i found you folded in the crepe myrtle

rerapturing every spring around the yard

remembered we tucked you

but here you've come

you new i'd surely recognize

i imagine it grows
box you
these small breasts

i've made this hollow
for you an alter

and what's hours, unfurls

grandmother
you always

spelled my name with an aura
(bee-aura-eye-tea-tea-in-why)

a halo of protection

that
crumpled everlasting
i felt the bough of
myself breaking
in a velvet lined bed
like a gem
back again as
knew beauty

this pine
left here beneath
my inheritance

heavy space
where what's
mines, yearns
into a linn of stardust

wadding like a life

preserver

only you new i was
an ancient

chant

only you new

the supremacy of our mother

mathematics—the
sacred ritual

of syllable and naming

grandmother
when i can't here you
you still follow
you eyelet of moon

i find myself knowing
faithfully
you hover of light

"My Great-Grandma"

I like to hear her lullabyes; I like to look in her looking-glass; I like to hear her babysitting stories. I like to play dress-up in her old-timy clothes and shoes; I like to look for her old pretty rings. I like to look at her old pictures and I loved her too!!!

She was the best great-grandma in the world and she never yelled at me. Even if she didn't know you she would talk to you and listen to you. And she would play with you, too! And I will always love Big Mama.

Brittny Ray

Brittny Ray

Discernment: An Heir/Loom

i know this by heart   like the dead
equations of my youth i used to dial a voice

this tightrope   coiled like an extension
cord   carries me   and i follow
all the way to my grandmother
's home

it tells me which trees to trust   and which to leave
alone   which water is safe to drink or wade
and which water a grave was made from

everything can be water if you're found in it face down

like the story of a distant cousin
left drowned in a field of cotton

like the uncle swimming while standing in the air
a veil of branches and spanish moss draping
his hair   the preacher slit six, seven times
in the stomach like small spaces for coins

my grandmother's father chasing haints
in the woods   how he died the death of a boxer
made sure all the blood they found
around him wasn't his own

Halloween: 2016

I didn't have a costume. Only the colored lights. Weak breath held in latex taped across the room.A red cup filled with vodka. A spit of juice. Thigh skin swelling the trellis of fishnet tights. A wanton witch. A slutty nurse. The warmth of liquor creeping on us. A flash flood. Daddy's tone to my ear on the phone. The city so small, I see his steps in the grass. They found him. He gone. The tender meat of his voice. The cry running back in reverse. The whole party comes. Drunk and surreal. A crowd grows. Some of them in masks. A boy disguised as Death takes down his hood. The body wheeled out in a bag. A honey locust pod. A spray of soft mist, patinaed over tears. Daddy kneads my shoulder. More comfort for him than me. To be one of so many children. To see them all swept away. Time lapse over flowers kneeling in a field.

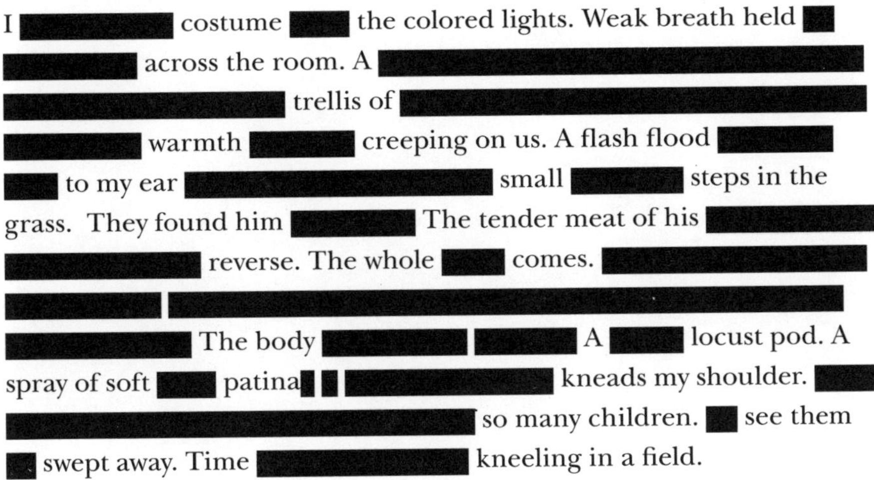

I costume the colored lights. Weak breath held
across the room. A
trellis of
warmth creeping on us. A flash flood
to my ear small steps in the
grass. They found him The tender meat of his
reverse. The whole comes.

The body A locust pod. A
spray of soft patina kneads my shoulder.
so many children. see them
swept away. Time kneeling in a field.

Only breath
creeping
in the grass.
The tender
surreal
mask ed
in honey

On Groceries

auntie they down here making nuggets and shit out of oxtails

they're just as high as when you left us higher
than that time you told me you had to rub your face
and body with snow to come down offa left hand cigarette
somebody had dipped in *that shit* and you didn't know it
you told me you could always tell if something wasn't natural
by the color and sound it made glowing

in between all your heavenly lists and obligations
as patron saint of chicken wing tips and big jokers
could you please petition that the white folks don't
grow too fond of smoked neck bones and country style
ribs lest the price of them reaches the hem of your garment
'cause they don't make good boosters like they used to
you know the ones that could steal the stank off boo boo
before it hit the commode and you know the Meat Man
don't even come around here no more or the Bbq Man
neither with his truck with the grill on the back of the trailer

now i'm too heaven minded to be a hater
but you know you really fucked the city up
leaving up outta here with so many recipes
even had the nerve to leave without teaching
me to make good gravy but for you
you know all things are forever
forgiven   god willing   next time i'm home
we bout to party out on Sheka porch
have a few drinks   let a little bit of sunlight hit us

and i know you don't care for the spooky shit
but if we made an altar for you
what should we put on it? a handle of Heaven
Hill? a little Bud Ice? a little souse, with the gristle in it?

Soul Glo

for Daddy (R.E.R.)

this is for the chain strangled in your daddy chest hair
the white cutlass red velvet
seats and interior the naked
lady silhouette floor mats the yellow
activator bottle in the console
for you

strolling your leather sandaled feet across the sea
of grandma's yard to the trailer
how you cleaved
it like the end of a rat tail comb
through thick hair with only the force of cool

black moses shifting the gravity
of grass beneath you
sheer Luther Vandross poise
i've seen sky since

but nothing like the one above your starry juiced head
to see the glint of cosmos roiled
in your curls as you lift me towards sky one handed

hint of bumpy bottle tanqueray in your glass too cool
to dance fuck those basketball shoes you mended
with carpenter's glue and the trifling niggas
that laughed at you not knowing you were a god
with his shirt open chains burrowed like gold lace
in the calligraphy of your chest hairs

walk with your hand bent back like money
will find you

Donna's House on Waterman: Texarkana, TX

i can't explain the cardinals i've seen of late
they kindle the trees like small glints of fire
spreading embers amidst the leaves from limb
to limb—but i know the space between us
is as thin as an eyelid and you said that red
birds were a loved one's rapture—a sign
that we all can somehow seep back beneath
the palimpsest and return. i learned this sitting
on the slab of your porch in sunlight. you blew a kiss
to a red bird hiding on a fence post, and when the kiss left
your lips it billowed out with cigarette smoke you must have been holding
in your throat like a last breath   it billowed like the ghosts we used to run
through on clotheslines when we were children living next door to that black
horse who would always run in circles before it rained and i can't
explain this being—at the crosshairs of memory with no safety
no solace in sight   only that this might be an answer
my ribcage is a haven for a resting red bird
she shimmers round the edges with smoke
i understand it now. i see the reason and agree.

ACKNOWLEDGMENTS

Highest praise and thanks to God and my Ancestors. To my dear husband Kenneth for your unwavering patience and sacrifice. Thank you for seeing about me and making sure I have fruit snacks and someone to hug when I'm afraid. I not only love you, I like you too. Gratitude to my babies, Iris and Lotus, for your patience and snuggles. I hope you're proud of Mommy because everything I do is out of love for you.

Gratitude to Mama and Daddy for your constant support and encouragement (Andy, your book should be next for real). To my sisters April, Dalphne, and Danielle for always showing up and leading the way for your little sister. I love y'all real bad. To TyTy, KeKe, Milly, MyMy, and Raheem: your Nannie/Unc/TaTa loves you so much. I hope this helps you remember those that came before you who loved you so much too. To Sheka, Chuck, and Baby Roni, thank you for sharing your sweet mama with all of us. So many of my favorite memories were with her and each of you. Love you more.

Love to all my Ray, Jackson, Greenwood, Ferrell, Matthis, and Wilkinson relatives and my Crowell family that loves me like they've always known me all along. Love to the memory of Kaladaa and Kyra. Special thanks to Dr. Joycelyn Williams Thomas for reminding me that my work has already spoken for me.

Thank you to the Soul Man and everyone on the *Ride or Die Hour*, which I listened to every Saturday while missing home and writing many of these poems. Peace to the memory of DeeDee Woods. Love to Macedonia, Wake Village, Texarkana, and Jefferson. To Doris Davis, Douglas Julien, Corinne Hinton, and Drew Morton at Texas A&M–Texarkana for your reassurance and support. Love to "Goody Nutter," Mrs. Murray, and all my former English teachers whose encouragement has never left me. Love to "The Flowers" and all my former colleagues at Texas High School who I still adore so much. Love to Monica "Sis" and Ricky Washington for always holding me down. Love to M.I.C Club forever. Love and light to the memory of Aaron Brand and Deanna Henderson.

Thank you to the former workers at the DAV on Griggs Street, my South Union neighbors, my former Pershing Middle School creative writing students, and the city of Houston for feeling like a second home. Love to LaQuandra "Bootz" Malveaux, whose work I look forward to soon.

My deepest appreciation to francine j. harris for your support and guidance, including the beautiful title of this book. Gratitude to Sarah Ehlers, Michael Snediker, and Nick Flynn for their encouragement throughout the process of creating this work. A special thank you to A. Van Jordan, whose work I have admired for so long, for acting as my external reader during the dissertation phase of this project. Thank you to Jason Berger, Martha Serpas, Audrey Colombe, Kavita Singh, Roberto Tejada, and Kevin Prufer for your influence and support during my time in the University of Houston Creative Writing program.

Gratitude to Ashley Warner and Jari Bradley for your invaluable friendship and the study groups that got me through. Thank you to Despy Boutris, Kaitlin Rizzo, Daniel Tompkins, Nick Rattner, giovanni singleton, Niki Herd, Erik Brown, and all my cohort members and friends who helped me through this process. Thanks to Chantal James and Lindsay Stewart for your kind consideration and feedback. Thank you to Courtney Stewart for believing in my work and helping me will this book into being. Love always to Ashli Herbert and Evan Seymour, two amazing writers whose sisterhood means everything to me.

Thank you to Lynne Thompson and the Napa Valley Writing Workshop, where several of these poems were written. Thank you to Jin Auh,

Jill Bialosky, Laura Mucha, Rivka Genesen, Pat Holl, and all those who participated in any way to bring this book into being.

Thank you to Opal Moore, Sharan Strange, and Dr. Donna Akiba Sullivan Harper for your warmth, influence, and encouragement. Love to SpelHouse and all my siblings in the AUC. Love to the memory of Clarence Stone and Tiffany McCollum-McLean. Peace and blessings to Dr. Georgene Bess Montgomery and all my colleagues and students who have welcomed me so warmly to Clark Atlanta University. Love and light to the memory of Dr. Timothy Askew.

NOTES

The last stanza of "I'm Not Here to Talk about the Rats or Roaches" is adapted from an excerpt from Neruda's *The Book of Questions.*

The interview poems are inspired by Marcelo Hernandez Castillo's interview form used in his work *Cenzontle.* Poet Chelsea DesAutel achieved a similar result during an installation in which she drew lines from poems at random as the answers to various questions. Some sections italicized in the interview poems come from a found document from my grandmother, Eunice Ferrell Matthis, detailing her confession of faith. The other italicized sections are excerpts from "Home," a video project featuring 8mm film taken by my grandfather, Robert Matthis. These excerpts contain responses from my mother, Andree Ray, and my sisters, April Matthis and Dalphne Ray Johnson, on their memories of home. The video project was featured in Obsidian's *Outta Sight: Sonic Bodies in the Galaxy of Black Listening* (issue 49.2).

In "Interview with an Ancestor III," "a noiseless uncalled for" is adapted from a line from Victoria Adukwei Bulley's poem "Luna."

In "Interview with an Ancestor IV," "Because you said poke sallet" was from a line of correspondence from Lori M. Miller. " Together is a mighty long time after all" is adapted from the title of Big K.R.I.T.'s album, *4eva Is a Mighty Long Time.*

“Nurse’s Log” begins as an erasure of the actual notes taken by hospice caretaker Patricia Williams on the day of my grandmother’s death.

In “Blood Petition” the line “the rituals fail to take” is from *Antigone.*

In “Things You Put in a Crown Royal Bag,” “three-eyed Ella, she does what I tella” and “tin top, roof don’t leak” refer to scoring 15 and 10 points in dominoes respectively.

The tracklist poems are a new form I call “grooves.” They open with a scene that’s set to the song in the title. Each line afterward, has the brevity of a song title. The time elements in the tracklist poems correspond to specific lyrics in the titles’ songs.

In “To the Tune of What’s a Telephone Bill by Bootsy Collins (Pt. II)” the lines “you inspire me (to poetry)” and “let me breathe” are from the song.

In “To the Tune of Give Me Your Love (Love Song) by Curtis Mayfield,” “hair shorter than a click on a 45” compares the length of hair to the short sound made when shooting the gun.

“Your Navel Cord’s Well” is a Black East Texas colloquialism based on the belief that newborns should not be allowed to cry due to the risk of umbilical hernia. Being allowed to cry or get upset means you’re old enough to cry without risk of injury, thus, “your navel cord’s well.” “The map of your palm waving” comes from a line from Natasha Trethewey’s poem, “Letter Home.”

In “I Dreamed My Name in Your Mouth with Pink Flowers,” the line “spelled my name with an aura” was based on a tweet from @damienxpat: “old southern black folk pronouncing ‘R’ like aura.”

In "Donna's House on Waterman: Texarkana, TX," the opening "*i can't explain the cardinals i've seen of late*" is after Janice Harrington's "Windshear."

Sincere thanks to the publications in which many of these poems first appeared:

"Down 59" and "Down 7th, Over East St." appeared online in *Cosmonauts Avenue* (2020).

"Blood Petition: A Prayer of Reckoning" appeared online in *Mount Island* (2020).

"Mama Voice" appeared online in *The West Review* (2020).

"Fasss" appeared in *Ploughshares* (2022).

"'Your Navel Cord's Well'" and "The Women I" appeared in *The Journal* (2021).

"Origin Tongues" (as "Derelict City of Our Origin") and "Notes on Your Absence" appeared online in *Aunt Chloe* (2020).

"32 Teeth" appeared online in *Hobart* (2022).

"How to Play Dead (Again)" appeared online in *Frontier* (2020).

A very early iteration of "How to Play Dead (Again)" was published in *Black Lives Have Always Mattered: A Collection of Essays, Poems, and Personal Narratives* (2Leaf Press, 2017).

"A Tether" appeared in *Copper Nickel* (2022).

"A Good Thing Found" appeared in *The Common* (2022).

"On Groceries" appeared online in *Swamp Pink* (2024).

"Soul Glo" appeared online in *Split Lip Magazine* (2022).

"Donna's House on Waterman: Texarkana, TX," "I'm Not Here to Talk about the Rats or Roaches," and "Scar Elegy" appeared online in *Triquarterly* (2024).